San Remo Italy Travel Tips

Discover the most up-to-date and amazing places to sleep, eat, and shop in the Liguria region (San Remo), along with essential information about the city

Hudson Miles

All rights reserved. No part of this publication may be reproduced, distributed, or transmitted in any form or by any means, including photocopying, recording, or other electronic or mechanical methods, without the prior written permission of the publisher, except in the case of brief quotations embodied in critical reviews and certain other noncommercial uses permitted by copyright law.

Copyright © (Hudson Miles) 2024

This pocket travel book which mainly focuses on **RECOMMENDATIONS** is a must-have when searching for the best places to stay, eat, and shop, along with their contact details. It also includes the city's affordable transport services and their phone numbers with essential information about the city and its Attractions.

Table Of Contents

San Remo

Attractions

Leisure Activities

Practical Information

Transport Services

Accommodation

Restaurants

Shopping

Phrases and Slang Terms

Liguria Region

Visa

If you are not a citizen of a European Union (EU) or Schengen Area nation, you will usually need a visa to enter Italy. The reason and duration of your stay may necessitate a different visa.

Requirements may vary based on the type of visa (tourist, work, study, etc.). Generally, you'll need a completed application form, passport, passport-sized photos, travel itinerary, proof of accommodation, financial means, and, depending on the visa type, additional documents

scan the QR code above

You can also download the visa application form, fill it out, print it, and take it to the Visa Application Centre for submission.
Refer to the details of the Tourist Office in this guide for additional personal information.

San Remo

Northwest Italy's Liguria region's Mediterranean coast is home to the commune (municipality) of Sanremo. Founded under the Roman Empire, this town of 55,500 people is a popular tourist attraction on the Italian Riviera. Numerous cultural events take place there, including the Milan-San Remo cycle race and the Sanremo Music Festival.

From the end of the 19th century until the middle of the 20th century, the beach town of Sanremo was a major social hotspot, and many of the opulent homes and hotels that still stand now serve as relics of that era.

The village is close to the French border and is one of Liguria's westernmost beach resorts in Italy. Although San Remo is the common term used to refer to it, Sanremo is its official name.

Even if it is no longer the primary haven for the affluent and attractive, the town is nevertheless a very enjoyable place to visit. Much of the attractiveness can be attributed to the small but charming old town and the fading elegance of the belle epoque homes.
Because the mountains shield the town from weather coming in from the north, San Remo has a fairly moderate and warm environment, which contributes to the town's growing popularity.

Wander around San Remo's mediaeval harbour, Porto Vecchio (the city now boasts a larger, more modern harbour). This small historic shoreline has a few restaurants along one side. This is assuming you are not racing to the little beach in the town centre, or that you are taking a break from the beach to see Sanremo town.

Once you've seen the harbour, take a leisurely stroll along the coastline and the main boulevards of the town centre, such as Corso degli Inglesi, to see some of the beautiful houses with their immaculate gardens. One of these magnificent homes, the Palazzo di Riviera, is home to the Tourist Office.

In addition, the 17th-century Santa Tecla Fort, which commands the majority of Sanremo's centre, can be seen between the tourism office and the shore. Situated in the western section of San Remo, the casino is the most famous building in the town and a superb example of Art Nouveau architecture.

Built in 1906, the casino is a popular tourist destination that serves as a witness to the prosperity of Sanremo's heyday. The theatre and café have also been added to the casino. Corso Matteotti, which is next to the casino, is one of San Remo's main shopping avenues.

The town's historic centre is located behind the port and along Corso Matteotti. It's mostly pedestrianised, fun to explore, and has lots of little streets to meander around.
The most fascinating part of our tour, in our opinion, was this neighbourhood known as "La Pigna" (translation: pinecone), which consists of tall mediaeval buildings grouped closely together along small pathways. This creates a dramatic contrast to the lavishness of the large residences.

Though visible from the street, the majority of Sanremo's most exquisite homes are private properties located east of the town centre. Corso Felice Cavallotti in the Giardini Nobel, a vast and exquisite garden directly behind the Newport area, is the ideal place to begin your investigation. Explore the stunning Villa Ormond grounds, which are situated across the street from this place.

These villas are too many for us to detail here, but you will be amazed at their opulence and range of architectural designs. Even the gardens are open for tours, but entry to the residences is limited. There's a tiny museum in the Palazzo Borea d'Olmo with local artefacts and artwork.

Alfred Nobel, who founded the Nobel Prize, resides in one of the elegant houses along this road that was originally owned by the musician Tchaikovsky.

Beaches Of Sanremo
Most people choose the beaches outside of Sanremo, like those at Bordighera, Taggia, and Bussana, unless they are just seeking a quick swim. Nonetheless, there are a few beaches in the town itself!

Churches
San Remo is not an exception to the rule that almost any popular Italian resort has a church—or several—to visit.

Located north of the main city, the Sanctuary of Madonna della Costa is one intriguing religious attraction that draws tourists. Constructed throughout the 17th and 18th century atop the town, it boasts an exquisite exterior in the baroque style.

The sanctuary, which was constructed on the site of an earlier church, has long served as a waypoint for sailors making their way back to the town across the river.

Church in the historic district of San Remo

Chiesa Russa Ortodessia, a Russian Orthodox church close to the San Remo Tourist Office, is another noteworthy house of worship in the area. At the height of San Remo's popularity, a Russian Tsarina settled here, and the chapel was constructed for the Russians who came after her. The most interesting aspect of the church is its interior, which has Russian icons.

The Cathedral of San Siro is a significant ecclesiastical structure in San Remo. Despite being founded in the twelfth century, the current Roman-style church was built or repaired primarily in the seventeenth century after the earlier church was damaged during a naval attack.

The City of Flowers, Sanremo
The "city of flowers," San Remo, celebrates the last Sunday of March with a procession adorned with floral decorations and live musical performances. If you live somewhere colder and would like to see some sunshine, now is a great time to visit; however, if you intend to attend the festival, make sure you reserve your lodging in advance as thousands of other people will be doing the same!

You may visit the Flower Market, which is reputed to be the biggest in Italy, at different times of the year. There are also lovely semi-tropical botanical gardens close by, some of which are right next to the villas, for those who enjoy gardening.

Taking a ride from San Remo to Milan
The renowned and intensely contested Milan to San Remo cycling race travels around 320 kilometres each year before reaching the town. This is held on the Saturday closest to March 19, so if you carefully

arrange a two-week visit, you may fit in both the bicycle race and the flower festival.

Many tourists like to visit the village of San Remolo, which is a few kilometres northwest of the town and offers breathtaking views over Sanremo and the surrounding countryside, to round out their tour of the town.

Situated a few kilometres northeast, Bussana Vecchia is, in our opinion, an especially lovely and fascinating location. This once-deserted village, full of charm and character, is today the centre of a bustling artistic community.

Transportation
The city is connected to Genoa and Ventimiglia, the centre of the French border, via the A10 motorway. The latter segment of it is commonly known as the Autostrada dei Fiori, or "Motorway of Flowers" There are many elevated areas that provide expansive views of the seashore along viaducts.

Between Ventimiglia and Menton, the A10 motorway merges with the A8 motorway in France. The numerous separate national routes that make up the European route E80. The A8 motorway has both free and toll-filled sections, just like the A10 motorway. Payment is not made until after passing through the Menton and Monaco municipalities when entering France from Italy.

The SS1, commonly known as the "Aurelia Bis," is a significant road that links Taggia with Sanremo. This bypass route is free of tolls. The coast road, also known as the SS1 or via Aurelia, traces the path of a Roman road.
This only has one lane in each direction for the majority of its journey near Sanremo, therefore it may get very crowded when it goes through villages. Taggia and Ventimiglia are connected to Sanremo via a trolleybus route that runs alongside the Aurelia.

The Côte d'Azur International Airport in Nice, France, is the closest airport to Sanremo and is 47 minutes away by vehicle. The city has train connections to Nice, Milan, Turin, Rome, Imperia, and Genoa, among other Ligurian cities.

In the past, the railway line ran along the coast, giving approaching traffic views. Faster trains are now possible due to the line's relocation further north and underground; the Sanremo railway station is now near City Hall. The former railroad line was renovated by the city and is now a pathway for bicyclists and pedestrians.

Along the way, it's easy to rent bicycles, and there are beaches to choose from on both routes out of San Remo. From Ospedaletti in the west to San Lorenzo al Mare in the east, the trail spans 25 kilometres.

Festivals and Events

Festival of music
Since 1950, the city of Sanremo's Ariston Theatre has played host to the renowned Sanremo Music Festival each year.

The 1956 Eurovision Song Contest, which is annually used to choose Italy's competitor for the European championship, was sparked by this festival. It was on this occasion in 1958 that Domenico Modugno debuted "Nel blu, dipinto di blu," which is now well known as "Volare" and gained widespread recognition.

Italians refer to the celebration as "Il Festival" (The Festival) because of its immense popularity. The Tenco Prize, an author song competition honouring Luigi Tenco, is held in the fall. Other events include the January/February Flowers Parade, where cities along the Italian Riviera design unique floral arrangements to be placed atop moving cars, evoking images of carnivals or Mardi Gras; and the summertime Ferragosto, also called the Firework International Contest.

The Festival is available for live viewing at the Ariston Theater or on television. Because the winter months bring good weather, exploring the city's beauties throughout the day is the best option if viewing the show in the evening is a must.

Carnival of Flowers in March
The annual March Corso Fiorito, often known as the Carnival of Flowers, and the San Remo Music Festival are two of the city's most popular events. However, the town is becoming more well-known and influential.

The second Mall Luxury Outlets facility in Florence, The Mall San Remo, opened its doors a few years ago in 2019. It's an open-air building overlooking the famous flower market in the neighbourhood and the sea. Though they are officially classified as malls, the stores provide carefully chosen and deeply reduced merchandise from labels like Gucci, Etro, Bottega Veneta, and Dolce & Gabbana.

Cuisines
Sanremo and the surrounding area is renowned for its mouth watering farinata, taranara, focaccia, focaccia alle cipolle, torta verde, e Taggiasca olives.

Arranging a trip to San Remo
It is easy to forget that this stretch of coastline is bordered by Italy until you arrive at Nice, France, the entry point to the well-known French Riviera hotspots of St. Tropez, Cannes, and Antibes. However, it's something to keep in mind, especially for San Remo, Italy, where, in the few days I spent exploring this hidden treasure, I could count on one hand the number of people who spoke English.

San Remo, on the Ligurian coast, is frequently eclipsed by its more glitzy French neighbours, even though it's only a short drive away. But don't expect to discover €205 seats at packed beach bars or any other picture-perfect moment here.

Beautiful, uncrowded botanical gardens, charming little fishing villages, and mouthwatering native Ligurian food may all be found in San Remo and the neighbouring environs. The opulent and historically noteworthy Grand Hotel San Remo and the Grand Hotel Del Mare in neighbouring Bordighera, which has lush grounds and a private beach, are two examples of upscale lodging options.

Even my non-shopping spouse was content to spend four hours at what is effectively an entertainment centre. (This is part of The Mall San Remo's objective to emphasise the destination as much as the shopping; you can use the complimentary concierge service to arrange for golf expeditions, boat tours, and olive oil tastings.)

Shopping Mall of Sanremo

That being said, the charming, historically significant Roman hamlet of Bussana Vecchia, home to seasonal artists, is just 10 minutes' drive from the opulent bubble of The Mall San Remo. A little further west are the beautiful public botanical gardens of Ventimiglia.

Last summer saw record numbers of travellers to Europe, so when we visited the UNESCO World Heritage Site Villa Hanbury during prime time, we were taken aback to see that it was almost completely empty. Numerous minor joys and delights can be found throughout the Italian Riviera, such as not having to wait in line, not bumping into people, fewer selfie sticks, and a generally more laid-back vibe.

Italy's Hanbury Gardens, Sanremo
There are lots of beach clubs, even on the Riviera's more relaxed side. However, for a genuinely local experience, we visited Ventimiglia's Le Calandre beach, where everyone seems to congregate after work due to the sandy shore and mild, blue waters. Because it lacks beach club amenities, this unexplored stretch of beach is free to use.

The Il Garroccio beach Italy's Bordighera, Sanremo

Though it was a sixth of the price of any beach club on the French side, my favourite beach belonged to a club named Il Carroccio and overlooked the gulf of Bordighera, a charming village right door to San Remo. Some of the cleanest beaches I've ever seen are found around this sea.

The nicest part is the always-available, wonderful, freshly made seafood pasta along with the warmth and friendliness that characterise Italian hospitality.

The yin and yang, or dualism, between the Italian and French sides and the switching between the two countries is what makes this site so beautiful. If you are looking for something fresh, you may take the train, as we did one evening in Ventimiglia, and get to Menton, the first town on the French side, in less than thirty minutes. You might have the lunch of a lifetime at Le Mirazur.

The interior of Sanremo, Italy's Mirazur
However, there's always good food to be found in San Remo. Visit San Remo just for the trofie pasta with Ligurian pesto at Il Giardino, the Royal Hotel San Remo's garden restaurant.

The Baccara Bistro Bello is the newest establishment in town. Baccara offers a contemporary take on local cuisine with dishes like eggplant carpaccio. With a beautiful floral wallpaper and a concealed patio that beckons during aperitivo, the restaurant has been remodelled to resemble a boutique hotel.

Situated near the city's historic port in the renowned fisherman's area, La Pignese is a San Remo tradition that was purchased by a family almost a century ago. A large assortment of fresh seafood is provided alongside classic Ligurian dishes like crab and rabbit ravioli.

Boating is another fun thing to do on the Riviera. Though there aren't many yachts in Italy, if you plan an excursion out of San Remo harbour, you will almost likely run into a funny, honest, and entertaining boat skipper. When it comes to discovering hidden swimming holes on the less-travelled Italian side of the border, San Remo and the more recent marina at Ventimiglia are excellent starting points. The marina is supposedly the brainchild of the developers of Monte Carlo and serves as "overflow parking" for seaborne traffic to Monaco.

My spouse and I couldn't believe no Americans were there, and we kept telling each other that.

My recommendation? Move ahead of them.

Here's how to make the most of your time in Sanremo and explore as much of the city as you can while still attending the Festival.

- **First Day: Ariston Theatre**

The Ariston Theatre Sanremo is great, but you can travel with confidence if you have the correct addresses. the initial stop? The Teatro Ariston, located on Via Giacomo Matteotti, is a must-see. Before coming to this site in 1977, the Festival was held in the Salone delle Feste del Casinò city.

However, don't forget to make a stop at the Co-Cathedral of San Siro, which is located on the street, en route to the City of Flowers' old theatre. Sanremo's oldest church is from the Romanesque era.
Ariston, 18038 Sanremo IM, Italy; 212 Giacomo Matteotti Avenue

- Casino

Proceed along Via Matteotti to the Casino, which is located on Via degli Inglesi, once the pictures have been taken. One of Italy's four casinos, it is housed in a liberty structure constructed by French architect Eugène Ferret. It is accessible to adults only and is open daily.

If you're paying attention, you've probably noticed that the Casino faces the distinctive domes of Santa Caterina, San Serafino di Sarov, Christ the Saviour, and other Orthodox churches. Constructed throughout the years 1912 and 1913, this renowned structure holds great significance for the city and boasts an intriguing past. Sanremo had a considerable Russian presence at the start of the 20th century, in part because Tsarina Maria Alexandrovna, the wife of Alexander II, was drawn to the Ligurian city. Even now, the Orthodox community uses it.

Corso degli Inglesi, 18, 18038 Sanremo IM Sanremo Casino, Italy

- La Pigna

Proceed to La Pigna, the city's named-for-its-shape historic core, after lunch. The city of Sanremo was founded around the year 1001, and the reason for its development was the persistent threat posed by Saracen pirates.

The Porta di Santo Stefano, which dates back to the thirteenth century, leads from Piazza Cassini to the Pigna. The Revolts of St. Sebastian covered tunnel is located here, on the left. It leads to the Piazza dell'Oratorio dei Dolori, an intricate network of narrow streets, steep slopes, and alleyways that is ideal for urban hikers.

La Pigna, the old heart of Sanremo, Italy, 18038 Sanremo IM

- **Day 2: Madonna della Costa Sanctuary**

This schedule calls for very comfy shoes on the second day. The Queen Elena Gardens are the main draw of the city and are located atop the Pigna. They were constructed starting in 1754 on the site of a Genoese fortress, but they also have historical roots dating back to the excavation of portions of the same Pigna during the Sanremo earthquake in 1887.

The ancient city centre's rooftops and the sea are both uniquely visible from the Gardens. They consist of several terraces joined by stairwells.

If you have made it this far, please take a moment to view Sanctuary Madonna della Costa, the city and location you are travelling to. It is said to have been constructed in observance of the feast of chains, on which the Sanremesi were honoured for having managed to free themselves from the feudal yoke of the Doria by being carried to the shrine of the chains.

Located at Piazzale Santuario Assunta, 15, 18038 Sanremo IM, Italy, lies the Madonna della Costa Sanctuary.

- Santa Tecla Fort

The schedule for the second day is completed in the most contemporary area of the city. After lunch, stroll the Empress Walk, browse the stores on Via Matteotti for a while, and then stop by one of the many eateries with a sea view for coffee or an aperitif.

You will encounter the Santa Tecla Fort, a sturdy and unflappable triangle-shaped building, as you wander toward the Old Port. Constructed in under 11 months, the Genoese formally opened it in March 1756, hoping to quell the rumours of the city's secession from the Republic of Genoa.

Giardini di Vittorio Veneto, 34 Santa Tecla Forte, 18038 Sanremo IM, Italy

- **Day 3: Sanremo's Villa Nobel**

The schedule for the third day similarly begins in the green. Other gardens in the city, such as those at Villa Nobel and Villa Ormond, are unquestionably worth visiting in addition to the Queen Elena Gardens.

Alfred Nobel, the man who invented the renowned Prize, lived in Villa Nobel. He spent the latter years of his life pursuing his scientific career in what he referred to as "my nest," her. It is now home to a functioning museum that has recreated Nobel's residence and surroundings. Beautiful gardens that anyone can visit for free.
After finishing that, spend at least an hour walking the walkways that border the river.

Alfred Nobel Nobel Gardens, 18038 Sanremo IM is the address in Italian.

- Villa Ormond

A second gem of the Ligurian city, Villa Ormond Park, is located on Corso Felice Cavallotti, 200 metres from Villa Nobel.
It is, in fact, nothing less. It's a peaceful, well-maintained sanctuary with many exotic species, ideal for leisurely walks.

Villa Ormond Corso 113, Felice Cavallotti, 18038 Sanremo IM, Italy

- Mercato Annonario

To find a special memento to cap off your day, stop into Mercato Annonario, which is open Monday through Saturday from 6 am to 1.30 pm.

Built in the middle of the 1950s, it provides much more than just a covered marketplace. In fact, zero kilometres is the place where you'll always find a few tiny local producers selling their specialties, which include crispy pizza known as sardenaira and olive oil and pesto.

Market announcement address: 5 Via Martiri della Libertà, 18038 Sanremo IM, Italy.

- **Day Four: Castelvecchi**

Do you have an intense love for two wheels? It is highly suggested that you ride the bike trail of the Riviera dei Fiori Coastal Park! Ospedaletti is reached by a direct 2-kilometre road from San Lorenzo al Mare that runs parallel to the coast. Take a bike rental in Sanremo and ride the cycling trail to San Lorenzo.

After travelling for roughly 11 kilometres, you will reach Bussana Vecchia, the fourth day's goal. This community is home to many artists and has a distinctive past.

The 1887 earthquake caused significant damage to the small town, and its residents fled. The village was so abandoned for many years that it earned the moniker "ghost town." But the town had a revival in the 1960s when some artists and craftspeople moved there.

With what remained of the debris, they rebuilt the hamlet and, in keeping with the hippy ethos, formed a kind of statute in which no one owned anything and everyone was a member of the community. It's practically a world away, the artists are still there, and a visit is well worth it.
Bussana Vecchia, Italy 18038 Bussana Vecchia IM

- **Day 5: Seborga**

On the fifth and last day of the program, travel 20 kilometres to Seborga, a picturesque mediaeval village located 20 kilometres from Sanremo. It's a little town with a wealth of traditions, history, and scenic beauty.

A short stroll from the town, the Church of San Martino is a little gem of Ligurian architecture. It is located next to the Palazzo dei Monaci, a mediaeval building that once housed the State Mint, where Prince George I struck the coins that still serve as the principality's emblem, the Luigini. Beneath its portico is a little drinking water source. After the walking tour, you should definitely check out the approximately 135 pieces created between 1700 and the present at the Museum of Musical Pieces. Once seated, sample the classic lasagna topped with pesto.
Head back the way you came, have a snooze by the water, and get ready to witness the Sanremo Festival Final as the schedule comes to a close. The winner ought to be the best man!
Italy's Seborga 18012, Seborga IM

Tour Sanremo, Liguria - Tatiana Gagarina Guida Turistica (Отдых в Италии)

Tourist information centre in Sanremo, Italy
Address: Via Privata Serenella, 46, 18038 Sanremo IM, Italy
Phone: +39 351 927 0001

Attractions

Below are more Attractions in the city, both popular and lesser-known ones. Visit any of them, depending on your preference.

- Passeggiata dell'Imperatrice: A charming pedestrian alley located along Lungomare Imperatrice, offering scenic views and a leisurely stroll by the sea.

- Via Crucis Monumentale: Experience historical significance at Corso degli Inglesi with the monumental Stations of the Cross.

- Palazzo Borea d'Olmo: Discover architectural beauty at Via Giacomo Matteotti, where Palazzo Borea d'Olmo stands majestically.

- Avvistamento Cetacei Sanremo: Encounter marine life excitement at Piazzale Lorenzo Vesco with whale watching opportunities.

- Piazza Colombo: Enjoy the bustling atmosphere of Piazza Cristoforo Colombo, a central square surrounded by shops and cafes.

- Piazza Eroi Sanremesi: Experience local culture at Piazza Eroi Sanremesi, a vibrant square with historical significance.

- Villa Ormond: Explore the historic Villa Ormond on Corso Felice Cavallotti, featuring a grand late-1800s building and expansive gardens.

- Palazzo Bellevue: Admire the panoramic views from Str. del Comune at Palazzo Bellevue, a stunning architectural gem.

- Statua di Mike Bongiorno: Pay homage to a television icon at Via Escoffier with the statue of Mike Bongiorno.

- Free Public Beach: Relax and soak up the sun at Pista Ciclabile del Parco Costiero della Riviera dei Fiori, offering a serene beachfront experience.

- Monumento Incas: Discover cultural intrigue at Piazza Cesare Battisti with the Monumento Incas.

- Fontana Artistica Monumentale dei Giardini Regina Elena: Marvel at artistic beauty at Via Tapoletti with the monumental fountain in the Giardini Regina Elena.
- Meridiana Analemmatica: Experience unique timekeeping at Sanremo, Province of Imperia, Italy, with the Meridiana Analemmatica.

- Piazzetta Oratorio dei Dolori: Find tranquility at Piazza Oratorio dei Dolori, a charming square featuring the Oratorio dei Dolori.

- Il Villaggio del Festival di Sanremo: Immerse yourself in music history at Corso Felice Cavallotti with the Festival di Sanremo Village.

- Casa Sanremo: Explore cultural heritage at Corso G. Garibaldi with Casa Sanremo, a historical landmark.

- Parco Marsaglia: Enjoy outdoor beauty at Corso Imperatrice with Parco Marsaglia, a picturesque park.

- Piazza Siro Carli: Experience local charm at Piazza Eroi Sanremesi, 94, con Piazza Siro Carli, a lively square.

- Porta San Giuseppe: Discover historical significance at Str. Borgo with Porta San Giuseppe, a well-preserved gate.
- Piazza Santa Brigida: Delight in the quaint ambiance at Vicolo Balilla, 1/59, with Piazza Santa Brigida, a charming square.

- Dolceacqua & the Nervia Valley: Explore the charming village of Dolceacqua, known for its Rossese wine and the picturesque bridge beloved by Monet.

Leisure Activities

Below are activities to get involved in, suggestions on day trips and excursions, Embark on any of these activities to enhance your travel experience.

- Pasta & Basta: Immerse yourself in the culinary delights of Sanremo with a pasta-making experience.

- Italian Market, Menton, Turbie Tour: Journey from Nice to experience the vibrant Italian market, Menton's beauty, and the scenic views of Turbie.

- Vespa Tour in Sanremo: Feel the breeze on a half-day Vespa tour, discovering the scenic spots of Sanremo.

- Day Hike in the Mountains of Sanremo: Lace up your hiking boots and trek through the breathtaking mountain landscapes surrounding Sanremo.

- Italian Market and Dolceacqua Full-day Tour: Enjoy a small-group tour from Nice, exploring Italian markets and the charming village of Dolceacqua.

- Private Full-Day Tour 3 Countries in 1 Day: Indulge in a luxurious private tour, visiting Italian markets, Menton, and Monaco in one unforgettable day.

- 1 Day Road Bike Tour of Ligurian Mountains: Embark on an adventurous road bike tour through the scenic Ligurian mountains.

- Sanremo Food Tour: Treat your taste buds to authentic Ligurian street food while exploring the mediaeval charm of Sanremo.

- Bussana: A Ghost Village Saved by Art: Discover the fascinating history of Bussana, a ghost village revived by artistry and creativity.

When travelling, it's advisable to book your tours in advance if interested. Consider using Viator for great deals. Scan the QR code to book online.

Travel Advice for Italy

Nobody likes to appear foolish
One of the most unpleasant experiences I've had while travelling was being warned by the police for eating ice cream in Piazza San Marco, Venice. simply because I had been so preoccupied with figuring out what to do in Venice.

Pack and Plan: Adapters, toiletries, travel documents, layers of clothing for variable weather, comfy walking shoes, and versatile pieces of clothing are essentials for any trip to Italy. It's crucial to travel light and refrain from overloading, choosing things that are both neutral and adaptable.

Packing can be made easier by researching the weather in advance and making clothing plans appropriately. It can be more convenient to travel with light clothing, a few jewellery items, and a roomy travel backpack or fanny pack. You can also prevent additional expenses by weighing your suitcase in advance and packing bulkier things for the airline.

General Info
Emergency Numbers: - Press 112 for assistance in all situations.
113 (thefts, accidents, and issues with the police).
- Fire Department: 115 (for weather-related issues and fire situations).
- Emergency Medical Care: 118 (for life-threatening illnesses or rescues from caves or mountains).
- 803.116 for Roadside Assistance (ACI).

Dial the international code +39 and then the number to make an Italian phone call.
- Dial 00, then the international code and number, to place an international call from Italy.
It is advised to get an Italian SIM card in order to communicate more affordably.

Budget Travel in Italy: Take low-cost airlines into smaller airports; take into account other modes of transportation, like high-speed trains connecting major cities.

To balance weather, costs, and to avoid the busiest times of the year, travel in May, June, September, and October, the shoulder seasons.

Using Public Transportation vs. Hiring a Car: Utilising public transportation is a more economical way to visit cities. Consider multi-day travel passes and buy your high-speed rail tickets in advance to save money.

Budget-Friendly Dining: Check out trattorias' fixed-price lunch menus for inexpensive lunch options.
Order your espresso at the bar to avoid additional service charges.
Fashion: Steer clear of the usual tourist outfit of sandals and white socks. Rather, dress tastefully and comfortably. **Cultural tip**: Cappuccinos are morning drinks; "caffe latte" is milk; and "Caffè shakerato" is iced coffee.

Avoid Getting a Cappuccino after 11am
It seems to interfere with your ability to digest.

Restaurant Hours: After lunch, restaurants close and reopen for dinner. However, bars and street food are open throughout the closures.
Electricity: Your electronics should include converters; use a two-pin European plug. **Shop and Service Hours**: In smaller cities and rural areas, especially, expect closures between 1 and 4 p.m.

City-Specific Advice: Pizza tastes peculiar to a city include "Pepperoni" (red peppers, not salami) and steer clear of Hawaiian pizza. Ask for the bill after lunch and be ready to have a long conversation.

Language: Acquire a few simple Italian expressions. It's possible that not everyone speaks English outside of tourist destinations.

Bathroom: Because bidets are so common in Italy, be conscious of their hygiene customs.

Savings Advice for Transportation:
ATM withdrawals can be made in Italian money if desired. When an ATM offers you the option to pay with your own money, it's a cunning ploy that leads to many travellers overspending. To save money and obtain the greatest deals, always opt to pay in the local currency, in this example, the euro.

Travel with budget airlines like **Vueling, EasyJet, Ryanair,** or **WizzAir.**

- Think about entering a city by land or travelling between cities on fast trains. As you go, buy tickets because train passes might not be the best deal. Examine point-to-point tickets and think about using the bus for some connections.

Local Transportation: - An extensive rail network connecting important Italian cities is maintained by **Trenitalia and Italo**.

- Areas not serviced by trains are covered by buses, while long-distance coaches are run by private companies like Flixbus.

- Coastal areas and islands are connected by ferries.

Driving in Italy: - If you're travelling through rural areas, renting a vehicle, motorcycle, or Vespa gives you more freedom.
- Roads are categorised into multiple groups with different speed limits.
- There could be potholes, traffic, and parking problems when driving.
Although they can occur, domestic flights are frequently less convenient than buses or railroads.
- Major cities are served by airlines including **Ryanair, easyJet, and ITA** Airways.
Cycling: There are bike paths all around Italy, some of which even accommodate electric bike options.
- Road cycling is very common in Northern Italy, especially in the Dolomites and Alps.
- Two websites that provide information on beaches and accessible facilities are **Village for All and Fondazione Cesare Serono.**

Websites and tools for reservations:
You'll discover everything you need for a smooth trip, from reliable lodging sites like **Booking.com, Plum Guide, Vrbo, and Airbnb** to necessary services like **Suntransfers** for airport transfers and **Trenitalia** for rail reservations. Learn insider advice on tour operators such as **Take Walks and Liv Tours** for unique experiences. Remember to download the suggested apps: **GetYourGuide, Viator, and Wanderlog** for browsing and booking tours and activities; **Omio or Skyscanner** for comparing and booking train, bus, and airline rates; and **Welcome Pickups** for airport

transfers. If you follow these crucial suggestions, your trip to Italy will be stress-free and unforgettable!

Travellers' Insurance:
For your vacation to Italy, we advise purchasing emergency medical insurance worth at least $50,000. **Medical Evacuation & Repatriation**: Pays for emergency transportation to a different hospital or, in the event that your treating physician determines that returning home is necessary for better care, to your country of origin.

Note that:
Petty theft is the major thing to watch out for when visiting Italy. Pickpocketing and bag snatching are two examples of these small-scale crimes that mostly happen in popular tourist destinations like Rome, Florence, and Venice.

Keep an eye out for valuables and leave pricey jewellery or watches at home. **Manners for Kissing a Cheek**: Italians frequently kiss one other on the cheek when mingling. Observe social cues; if you feel uncomfortable, a simple handshake will suffice.

Scan the QR code below and search for the Location you are going to in Italy and have a better view. Safe travels.

The map is the same on your phone. Consider taking screenshots as you walk around with no connection needed. Alternatively, you can contact the tourist office using the addresses and numbers provided in this guide.

In most cases, I use the Wanderlog site or app to plan my trip itinerary and expenses. You can try it if you're interested. Scan the QR code to learn more.

Transportation

Below are recommended Transportation related services in the city. It is advisable to make reservations online at the **Omio** site or by scanning the QR code.

Transport Services

Below are recommended transportation-related services in the city. Contact them if necessary upon landing at the nearby airport. It is advisable to make reservations online at the omio site or by scanning the QR code above.

- Taxi Sanremo: A reliable taxi service located at Via Giorgio Pallavicini, offering transportation assistance with a phone number: +39 0184 541454.

- Radiotaxi: Conveniently situated at Piazza Cristoforo Colombo, Radiotaxi provides taxi services with a contact number: +39 0184 541454.

- Universo Srl: A trucking company operating from Via Quinto Mansuino, providing transportation services with a phone number: +39 0184 461200.

- Taxi: Another taxi service available at Corso Augusto Mombello, offering transportation solutions with a contact number: +39 0184 572203.

- Franco Trasporti: A mover service located at Via Galileo Galilei, offering transportation assistance with a contact number: +39 377 096 4133.

- Autostazione a Sanremo: A transportation service located at Via Bartolomeo Asquasciati, serving as a bus station in the area.

- Riviera Trasporti Spa: A bus company situated at Corso Felice Cavallotti, providing bus transportation services with a contact number: +39 0184 592711.

- Trasporti MEC Service: A trucking company offering transportation solutions, reachable at +39 351 314 0782.

- Capolinea Autobus Coldirodi: A transportation service located at Via Umberto, serving as a bus stop.

- Autostazione RT - Sanremo Bus Station: A bus ticket agency situated at Piazza Cristoforo Colombo, providing bus ticketing services with a contact number: +39 0184 592707.

- Taxi: Another taxi service available with a contact number: +39 0184 572202.

- Capolinea Bus San Lorenzo: A transportation service serving as a bus stop in Sanremo.

- Radio Taxi: A taxi service located at Corso Nazario Sauro, providing transportation assistance with a contact number: +39 0184 541454.

- Casello Autostradale Sanremo: A toll booth located at Via Monte Ortigara, offering toll collection services on the highway.

Accommodation

When travelling, it's advisable to book your hotel in advance.

Consider using bookings for great deals, available for registered hotels worldwide. Scan the QR code to book online. Here are some recommended hotels to consider:

- Royal Hotel Sanremo
  - Location: Corso Imperatrice, 80
  - Phone: +39 0184 5391

    Elegant sea-view lodging with dining, spa, outdoor pool, and tennis court for a refined stay.

- Hotel de Paris Sanremo
  - Location: Corso Imperatrice, 66
  - Phone: +39 0184 520725

    Art Nouveau style suites with fitness room, spa, and panoramic sea views for luxurious comfort.

- Hotel Belsoggiorno Sanremo
  - Location: Corso Matuzia, 41

- Phone: +39 0184 667631

Unpretentious neoclassical hotel offering complimentary breakfast, parking, and loaner bikes for a relaxed stay.

- Grand Hotel de Londres
  - Location: Corso Matuzia, 2
  - Phone: +39 331 150 5721

Quaint 19th-century hotel with restaurant and outdoor pool offering warm, comfortable accommodations.

- Hôtel Napoléon
  - Location: Corso Guglielmo Marconi, 56
  - Phone: +39 0184 662244

Simple hotel with bright rooms, terraces, and free parking for a hassle-free stay near the sea.

- Hotel Villa Maria
  - Location: Largo Nuvoloni, 30
  - Phone: +39 0184 531422

Relaxed lodging with complimentary amenities like parking, Wi-Fi, and breakfast, plus a cosy bar and lounge.

- Sanremo Luxury Suites
  - Location: Corso Imperatrice, 77
  - Phone: +39 0184 667881

Classic hotel offering comfortable rooms, casual dining, and complimentary breakfast for a laid-back stay.

- Grand Hotel Des Anglais
  - Location: Salita Grand Albergo, 134
  - Phone: +39 0184 667840

Classic Belle epoque hotel with free amenities like breakfast, parking, and Wi-Fi for a comfortable stay.

- Miramare the Palace Hotel
  - Location: Corso Matuzia, 9
  - Phone: +39 0184 667601

Cosy rooms and suites with sea-view garden gazebo for a tranquil retreat by the sea.

- Hotel Paradiso
  - Location: Via Roccasterone, 12
  - Phone: +39 333 488 0168
  Casual hotel with restaurant, sea views, pool, and private beach for a relaxing coastal getaway.

- Hotel Principe
  - Location: Via Privata Asquasciati Fratelli, 96
  - Phone: +39 0184 531919
  Simple accommodations with restaurant, pool, and free parking for a convenient stay.

- Hotel Villa Sophia
  - Location: Corso Matuzia, 21
  - Phone: +39 0184 667234
  Casual hotel in a former convent offering dining, bar, and proximity to the beach for a tranquil stay.

- NYALA SUITE HOTEL
  - Location: Str. Solaro, 134
  - Phone: +39 0184 667668
  Modern hotel with warm rooms, outdoor pool, casual dining, and bar for a comfortable stay.

- Hotel Bobby Executive

- Location: Corso Guglielmo Marconi, 208
  - Phone: +39 0184 660255

Laid-back hotel with restaurant, bar, indoor pool, and complimentary amenities for a relaxed stay.

- Lolli Palace
  - Location: Corso Imperatrice, 70
  - Phone: +39 0184 531496

Polished villa hotel offering Italian dining, rooftop garden, and sea views for a serene experience.

- Hotel Rio
  - Location: Corso Matuzia, 84
  - Phone: +39 0184 662273

Straightforward accommodations with complimentary Wi-Fi and breakfast for a hassle-free stay.

Restaurants

Try any of the top recommended restaurants known for their pleasant services, mouthwatering menus, and reasonable prices. You can reach them through the provided contact details.

- Il Rustichello
  - Location: Vicolo dei Gherzi, 34
  - Phone: +39 388 652 3870

    Authentic Italian trattoria featuring Ligurian specialties like Trofie al Pesto, freshly prepared with traditional ingredients.

- Soul
  - Location: Corso Augusto Mombello, 41
  - Phone: +39 0184 638172

  Cosy restaurant offering Mediterranean cuisine, including Farinata, a crispy chickpea pancake baked to perfection.

- Ristorante Mare Blu
  - Location: Via Carli, 5
  - Phone: +39 0184 535680

  Charming seaside eatery serving Cima alla Genovese, tender veal breast stuffed with a savoury mixture.

- Osteria del Marinaio
  - Location: Via Gaudio, 30
  - Phone: +39 0184 533354

  Traditional Italian osteria specialising in Frittura di Pesce, lightly fried seafood showcasing the region's flavours.

- VN - Villa Noseda Sanremo
  - Location: Corso degli Inglesi, 1
  - Phone: +39 335 186 1905

  Elegant seafood restaurant offering Cappon Magro, a festive dish with layers of fresh seafood and green sauce.

- Ristorante Vela D'Oro
  - Location: Via Gaudio, 9
  - Phone: +39 0184 504302

   Intimate Italian restaurant known for its Torta Pasqualina, a savoury pie filled with ricotta cheese and Swiss chard.

- Gilda
  - Location: Via Nino Bixio, 53
  - Phone: +39 0184 199 1778

   Quaint trattoria serving Panigacci con Pecorino e Salumi, savoury pancakes with cured meats and local cheese.

- Ristorante Buena Vista
  - Location: Corso degli Inglesi, 15
  - Phone: +39 0184 509060

   Argentinian restaurants offering hearty dishes like Trofie al Pesto, prepared with a South American twist.

- La Bodeguita Sanremo
  - Location: Via Gaudio, 16
  - Phone: +39 379 236 6209

   Lively eatery featuring Acciughe al Verde, anchovies marinated in a tangy parsley and garlic sauce.

- Solentiname
  - Location: Lungomare Vittorio Emanuele II
  - Phone: +39 0184 664477

Italian restaurant offering classic dishes like Focaccia, a Ligurian bread topped with olive oil and rosemary.

Shopping

Below are recommendable shops in the city.
Explore shopping in any of these stores and bring back some souvenirs.

- San Remo
  - Type: Shopping mall
  - Address: Piazza Eroi Sanremesi, 3
  - Phone: +39 348 254 9339
  Large shopping centre offering a variety of stores for in-store shopping convenience.

- The Mall Sanremo
  - Type: Outlet mall

- Address: Via Armea, 43
  - Phone: +39 0184 196 8968

Outlet shopping destination featuring a range of discounted fashion and lifestyle brands.

- Gucci outlet
  - Type: Shopping mall
  - Address: Via Armea, 53
  - Phone: +39 0184 512563

Premium outlet store offering upscale Italian fashion and accessories from the renowned brand.

- Royal Gift Shop
  - Type: Boutique
  - Address: Corso Imperatrice, 80
  - Phone: +39 0184 5391

Boutique specialising in unique gifts and souvenirs, offering in-store shopping, pickup, and delivery options.

- Borgo Sas Di Di Gregorio R. E Ferrero C. & C.
  - Type: Shopping mall
  - Address: Via Galileo Galilei, 419
  - Phone: +39 0184 592163

Small shopping complex providing various retail options for shoppers.

- Dieng Idrissa

- Type: Shopping mall
  - Address: Via Martiri della Libertà, 14
  - Phone: +39 0184 635492

  Shopping destination offering a selection of stores for in-store shopping convenience.

- Dho & D'Alberto Snc Di Ettore Dho Emaurizio D'Alberto
  - Type: Shopping mall
  - Address: Via della Repubblica, 90
  - Phone: +39 0184 508407

  Retail complex featuring a small number of shops for in-store shopping needs.

- Centro Commerciale Italia - GrIn WebS
  - Type: Store
  - Address: Via Francesco Corradi, 88
  - Phone: +39 348 857 9299

  Retail stores offering various products and goods for shoppers.

- Shopping
  - Type: Clothing store
  - Address: Via Giacomo Matteotti, 84
  - Phone: +39 0184 543031

  Apparel stores provide a range of clothing options for shoppers.

- Hyper Market S.R.L.
  - Type: Shopping mall
  - Address: Corso Guglielmo Marconi, 140
  - Phone: +39 0184 189 2634

  Large retail centre offering a diverse selection of goods and products for shoppers.

- Bottega Veneta Sanremo The Mall Outlet
  - Type: Leather goods store
  - Address: Via Armea, 43/UNITA' V
  - Phone: +39 0184 183 0070

  Outlet store specialising in upscale Italian leather goods and fashion items.

- EMPORIO APRICOT Abbigliamento Sanremo Multibrand & Made in Italy
  - Type: Clothing store
  - Address: Via Debenedetti, 29
  - Phone: +39 393 552 3842

  Multibrand clothing store offering a variety of Italian-made fashion items for shoppers.

- Spinnaker Boutique - Sanremo
  - Type: Clothing store
  - Address: Via Giacomo Matteotti, 141
  - Phone: +39 0184 505550

  Boutique clothing store providing a curated selection of fashion items for shoppers.

Phrases and Slang Terms

Basic Italian phrases and area slang terms to be familiar with before travelling.

- Buongiorno! - Good morning!
- Buonasera! - Good evening!
- Ciao! - Hello/Hi!
- Arrivederci! - Goodbye!
- Grazie! - Thank you!

- Prego! - You're welcome!
- Per favore! - Please!
- Mi scusi! - Excuse me!
- Parla inglese? - Do you speak English?
- Posso avere il conto, per favore? - Can I have the bill, please?

- Dove si trova il bagno? - Where is the bathroom?
- Quanto costa? - How much does it cost?
- Posso pagare con carta di credito? - Can I pay with credit card?
- Vorrei prenotare una tavola per due persone. - I would like to book a table for two.
- Vorrei ordinare. - I would like to order.
- Che cosa mi consiglia? - What do you recommend?

- Vorrei una birra/vino/acqua. - I would like a beer/wine/water.

- Mi piacerebbe mangiare qualcosa di tipico italiano. - I would like to eat something typical Italian.
- Posso avere il menu, per favore? - Can I have the menu, please?
- Questo è molto buono! - This is very good!
- Dove posso trovare un bancomat? - Where can I find an ATM?

- A che ora chiude il negozio? - What time does the shop close?
- Mi può aiutare a trovare un taxi? - Can you help me find a taxi?
- Come posso arrivare in centro città? - How can I get to the city center?

- Mi può chiamare un taxi? - Can you call me a taxi?
- Ho prenotato una camera. - I have a reservation for a room.
- Dove si trova la stazione ferroviaria/autobus? - Where is the train/bus station?
- Qual è il numero di emergenza? - What is the emergency number?
- Ho bisogno di aiuto. - I need help.
- Mi sono perso/a. - I am lost.

- Dove posso trovare una farmacia? - Where can I find a pharmacy?

- Sto cercando un ristorante. - I am looking for a restaurant.
- Posso prendere un taxi qui? - Can I take a taxi here?
- Vorrei una mappa della città. - I would like a map of the city.

- Ho una prenotazione. - I have a reservation.
- Mi potrebbe consigliare un buon ristorante? - Could you recommend a good restaurant?
- Posso usare il suo telefono? - Can I use your phone?
- Mi potrebbe dire dov'è la spiaggia più vicina? - Could you tell me where the nearest beach is?
- Dove posso noleggiare una bicicletta? - Where can I rent a bike?

- Vorrei acquistare un biglietto per il museo. - I would like to buy a ticket for the museum.
- A che ora inizia il concerto? - What time does the concert start?
- C'è un mercato qui vicino? - Is there a market nearby?
- Dove posso acquistare souvenir? - Where can I buy souvenirs?

- Ho perso il mio bagaglio. - I have lost my luggage.
- Mi può aiutare con le indicazioni? - Can you help me with directions?

- Vorrei noleggiare una macchina. - I would like to rent a car.
- Dov'è la stazione dei treni? - Where is the train station?
- Dov'è il bagno pubblico più vicino? - Where is the nearest public restroom?
- C'è un supermercato qui vicino? - Is there a supermarket nearby?
- Posso pagare in contanti? - Can I pay in cash?

- È incluso nel prezzo? - Is it included in the price?
- Qual è il modo migliore per arrivare in centro città? - What is the best way to get to the city center?
- Vorrei cambiare dei soldi. - I would like to exchange some money.
- Che ore sono? - What time is it?
- Quanto tempo ci vuole per arrivare all'aeroporto? - How long does it take to get to the airport?

- Posso fare una prenotazione? - Can I make a reservation?
- Ho una allergia alimentare. - I have a food allergy.

- Vorrei ordinare da asporto. - I would like to order takeaway.
- Dove posso trovare un medico? - Where can I find a doctor?

- Ho bisogno di un taxi per domani mattina. - I need a taxi for tomorrow morning.
- È incluso il servizio in camera? - Is room service included?
- Posso avere un'altra coperta? - Can I have another blanket?
- C'è un deposito bagagli? - Is there a luggage storage?

- Vorrei chiamare un taxi. - I would like to call a taxi.
- C'è un internet café qui vicino? - Is there an internet café nearby?
- A che ora si apre il museo? - What time does the museum open?
- Dove posso trovare informazioni turistiche? - Where can I find tourist information?

- Posso avere il tuo numero di telefono? - Can I have your phone number?
- Qual è il tuo nome? - What is your name?
- Posso sedermi qui? - Can I sit here?

- Dove posso trovare una lavanderia self-service? - Where can I find a self-service laundry?
- Posso avere un'altro cuscino? - Can I have another pillow?

- Vorrei fare il check-out. - I would like to check out.
- Vorrei prenotare un tour. - I would like to book a tour.
- Mi potrebbe dare indicazioni per arrivare alla stazione dei treni? - Could you give me directions to the train station?
- Posso avere una carta della città? - Can I have a city map?

- Ho bisogno di un taxi per stasera. - I need a taxi for tonight.
- Sto cercando un albergo economico. - I am looking for a budget hotel.
- Vorrei fare una prenotazione per due persone. - I would like to make a reservation for two people.
- C'è un ristorante aperto a quest'ora? - Is there a restaurant open at this hour?

- Sto cercando un negozio di souvenir. - I am looking for a souvenir shop.
- Vorrei noleggiare uno scooter. - I would like to rent a scooter.

- C'è una piscina in the hotel? - Is there a swimming pool in the hotel?
- Qual è il tuo indirizzo email? - What is your email address?
- Posso avere un'altra chiave della camera? - Can I have another room key?
- Come si chiama questo piatto in italiano? - What is this dish called in Italian?
- Potrebbe scattarmi una foto, per favore? - Could you take a photo of me, please?
- Mi può consigliare un buon gelato? - Can you recommend a good gelato?

- C'è un parcheggio gratuito qui vicino? - Is there free parking nearby?
- Quale è la specialità locale? - What is the local specialty?
- Vorrei visitare un mercato. - I would like to visit a market.

- Qual è il miglior ristorante di pesce qui vicino? - What is the best seafood restaurant nearby?
- Posso avere il menu in inglese? - Can I have the menu in English?
- Ho bisogno di un ombrello. - I need an umbrella.
- Dove posso trovare un distributore di benzina? - Where can I find a gas station?
- Qual è il codice Wi-Fi? - What is the Wifi code?

- Vorrei prenotare un taxi per domani sera. - I would like to book a taxi for tomorrow evening.
- Posso avere un po' di sale, per favore? - Can I have some salt, please?
- Posso avere il tuo numero di telefono? - Can I have your phone number?
- Come si dice "grazie" in italiano? - How do you say "thank you" in Italian?

- Vorrei fare una prenotazione per un tour della città. - I would like to make a reservation for a city tour.
- Mi potrebbe consigliare un buon ristorante di cucina tradizionale italiana? - Could you recommend a good restaurant for traditional Italian cuisine?

- Sto cercando un negozio di souvenir per portare a casa qualche ricordo. - I'm looking for a souvenir shop to bring back some memories.
- Potrebbe raccontarmi qualcosa sulla storia di Sanremo? - Could you tell me something about the history of Sanremo?
- C'è qualche evento o festa locale oggi? - Is there any local event or festival today?
- Vorrei prenotare un taxi per l'aeroporto domani mattina. - I would like to book a taxi to the airport tomorrow morning.

- Mi potrebbe aiutare a trovare un hotel con una vista sul mare? - Could you help me find a hotel with a sea view?

- Sto cercando un ristorante romantico per una cena speciale. - I'm looking for a romantic restaurant for a special dinner.
- Potrebbe consigliarmi un buon gelato artigianale? - Could you recommend a good artisanal gelato?
- Dove posso trovare un mercato all'aperto per fare un po' di shopping? - Where can I find an outdoor market for some shopping?

- Vorrei noleggiare una bicicletta per esplorare la città. - I would like to rent a bike to explore the city.
- Cosa devo visitare assolutamente durante il mio soggiorno a Sanremo? - What must I absolutely visit during my stay in Sanremo?
- Vorrei prenotare un tavolo per questa sera per una festa di compleanno. - I would like to book a table for tonight for a birthday party.
- Mi potrebbe dare indicazioni su come raggiungere il centro storico? - Could you give me directions on how to reach the historic center?
- Sto cercando un posto tranquillo dove rilassarmi e godermi il panorama. - I'm looking for a quiet place to relax and enjoy the view.

- Vorrei sapere quali sono le spiagge più belle della zona. - I would like to know which are the most beautiful beaches in the area.

- Vorrei prenotare un corso di cucina per imparare a preparare piatti italiani. - I would like to book a cooking class to learn how to prepare Italian dishes.
- Mi potrebbe dire quali sono le attrazioni principali per i bambini in città? - Could you tell me what are the main attractions for children in the city?

- Vorrei noleggiare un'auto per esplorare i dintorni di Sanremo. - I would like to rent a car to explore the surroundings of Sanremo.
- Dove posso trovare informazioni sulle escursioni nei dintorni di Sanremo? - Where can I find information about excursions around Sanremo?

Slang Terms
- Ciao bello/bella - Hey handsome/beautiful
- Che palle! - What a pain!
- Dai! - Come on!
- Figo/a - Cool
- Che fico! - How cool!
- Dai su! - Oh, come on!
- Mi raccomando - Take care
- Magari! - I wish!
- Che casino! - What a mess!

- Allora - So, well
- Che schifo! - How disgusting!
- Non c'è problema - No problem
- Vabbè - Whatever

- Mannaggia - Darn it
- Figurati - Don't mention it
- Accidenti! - Darn!
- Che casino! - What a mess!
- Ma dai! - Oh, come on!
- Dai un'occhiata - Have a look
- Che ridere! - How funny!
- Boh - I don't know

- Ci vediamo dopo - See you later
- Che fregatura! - What a rip-off!
- Ma che dici? - What are you saying?
- Che palle! - What a drag!
- Perbacco! - Wow!
- Mettere le mani avanti - To cover one's back
- Che dell'affare! - What a great deal!
- Andare a ruba - To sell like hotcakes

- Fare il passo più lungo della gamba - To bite off more than one can chew
- Fare bella figura - To make a good impression
- Fare fiasco - To fail

- Rimanere a bocca asciutta - To be left with nothing
- Dare una mano - To lend a hand
- Tirare il pacco - To stand someone up

- Prendere in giro - To make fun of
- Fare ciao ciao - To say goodbye
- Farsi le seghe mentali - To overthink
- Avere la pappa pronta - To have everything easy
- Dare il bianco - To ignore someone
- Dare il benservito - To kick someone out
- Fare la spia - To snitch

- Andare a fuoco - To be on fire (figuratively)
- Dare una testata - To headbutt
- Stare a galla - To stay afloat
- Scoppiare dalle risate - To burst out laughing
- Avere le mani bucate - To be a spendthrift
- Avere le palle - To be brave

Liguria

Welcome to Liguria, the region that is home to the Italian Riviera and a definite must-visit in Europe. After falling in love with this region of Italy during a city break to Genoa last summer, I have been going there for years. If you're looking for somewhere fresh to visit, it's a great alternative to the Amalfi Coast or Puglia.

Liguria's Location

A region on Italy's northwest coast, Liguria is sandwiched between Tuscany, Emilia-Romagna, and Piremont. The Ligurian Sea envelops the port town of Genoa, which serves as the region's capital.

Beautiful beaches, port towns, fishing villages, and crystal-clear water define the region. Green hills and valleys can be found inland, making them ideal for exploring and trekking.

The region is covered in vineyards and olive groves, which contribute to Italy's delicious cuisine.

Which season is ideal for travelling to Liguria?

The Ligurian Coast is best visited in the summer, as it is in most of the Mediterranean. I would advise travelling between June and September just outside of these busy times, as July and August in particular may get very hot and crowded. There will be fewer visitors in May and October, when pleasant, warm weather is expected with the possibility of sporadic showers of rain.

I wouldn't advise visiting this area in the winter because it can get rather stormy from November to March, and many of the hotels and restaurants are closed during this time. stormy in the winter.

Shoulder season, which runs from April to May, is a great time to visit Liguria if you want to take advantage of low hotel and airfare prices. Be prepared for all kinds of weather during this time of year!

Travel Tips

By air: There are numerous European flights from Genoa's respectable international airport. There are 1-2 daily flights available to London throughout the year. There are flights from Manchester to Liguria for people in the UK's north.

By train: I would advise using the well-connected rail system to travel between the towns and villages. With direct trains to Milan, Nice (in France), Rome, and numerous other major Italian towns, Genoa is the main terminus. You can reach the shore from Genoa, which is home to communities like Santa Margherita, La Spezia, Camogli, and the Cinque Terre settlements.

By car: There are a lot of great places in Italy for a road trip, if that's what you're looking for. As you travel along stunning coastal roads, past picture-perfect villages, across hills, and across mountains, roll down your windows and take in the warm breeze. The fastest route is the autostrada, which stretches from east to west and provides breathtaking views as well.

A few things to consider when visiting this area:

Open an Easy Parking account if you drive. Since this will enable you to adjust the parking period if you intend to stay somewhat longer.

Settle into private beach beds. The majority of the beach's excellent areas are private, despite the excellent facilities.

Take advantage of the free white parking bay if you find one. The blue lines are compensated. Yellow lines are intended only for loading and for handicapped users.

Dishes in Liguria

Focaccia Genoese: Its dough is unleavened, baked at a temperature of 520°F to 570°F, and it is no taller than 1 inch.

Focaccia di Recco: Cheese-filled, crunchy, and thin.

Farinata: a nutritious dish cooked with olive oil and chickpea flour.

Panissa: A tasty and easy fried chickpea polenta.

Trofie with pesto: A classic and delectable pasta dish with a rich Genoese pesto sauce.

Rabbit in the Ligurian style: delicate rabbit paired with pine nuts and olives.

Corzetti: Medallions of pasta imprinted with the family crest, typically served with walnut sauce.

Pansotti: Walnut sauce-covered stuffed pasta topped with wild greens.

Gobeletti di Rapallo: Quince jam-filled shortcrust pastry.

Reminiscent of Baci di Dama, Baci di Alassio are hazelnut and chocolate pastries filled with chocolate ganache.

Best locations in Liguria
The locations that are worth visiting are listed below. They are ranked according to the popular ones. Choose the one you can cover based on how long you have.

- Cinque Terre

To get to Cinque Terre, drive to the train station in La Spezia. The five villages that make up Cinque Terre are all reachable by train. All five villages are accessible with a daily pass. The beach at Monterosso is good. You have two options: travel the opposite route and see every village before arriving in Monterosso to enjoy the beach. We took a different approach, and it felt really good.

- Noli Noli

There are fantastic private beaches with immaculately clear water in this charming mediaeval town. There's a good length of beach. Thus, you may locate a quiet spot even during busy times of year. You can tour the town after relaxing on the beach. It features a café and a few specialty small shops. Your entire day will be over quickly.

- Pisa

It's time to take in the sights after a long day at the beach. Discovering the marvel that is the Leaning Tower of Pisa would be a wonderful place to start. You'll notice as you go to Pisa how the hills give way to the stunning Tuscan countryside. If your taste senses need a rest, a Mc Donald's is on the way.

- Ligure

The region's longest stretch of sandy beach is found near Finale Ligure. Every segment is essentially the same. There's no shortage of kid-friendly activities. Your children will adore it.

- Marina Diano

Diano Marina offers a fantastic nightlife that is ideal for families. plenty of eateries and cafeteria options. If you want to enjoy the evening, I would suggest spending the night here. The Hotel Metropole is an excellent choice if you intend to stay here. The motel offers free on-site parking. Additionally featured is a private beach. The beach amenities are excellent. All beach gear, including tubes and floating beds, is available for free.

Bon Voyage

Printed in Great Britain
by Amazon